Monasticism:
Patterns of Piety

By Justo L. González

Contents

D1516846

1
A Piety of Flight

A Piety for Its Time

It was an exhilarating time. After two and a half centuries during which persecution was always a threat and often a tragic reality, a new age was opening for the Christian church. Emperor Constantine had put an end to persecution, and during his reign he had shown increasing favor toward Christians. In A.D. 325, upon imperial invitation and at imperial expense, over three hundred bishops from various parts of the church had gathered at Nicaea to discuss weighty theological questions as well as administrative matters. Constantine himself was later baptized on his deathbed.

After that time, with very few exceptions—the most notable one was Constantine's nephew Julian—the rulers of the Empire would call themselves Christian. Favors and privileges were showered on the church and its leaders. The old notion that Christianity was the uncouth faith of the ignorant and of the lower classes rapidly disappeared. Soon only a die-hard core of aristocratic pagans who bemoaned the passing of the old order held an unfavorable view of Christianity. Sumptuous places of Christian worship were being built, and the ancient pagan temples were losing both their appeal and their financial backing. People were flocking to the baptismal waters, often led by respected imperial officers. In a few years the ancient religions would be little more than a distant memory, surviving only in isolated outposts where new currents had little impact and in small pockets of aristocratic traditionalism.

However, it was also a dangerous time. During the previous two and a half centuries, Christians had learned that after experiencing relatively easy times, believers often had difficulty facing persecution with fortitude. In periods of persecution Christians prepared themselves for the ultimate test; and when that test actually came, few were willing to deny their faith in order to save their lives. But when an entire generation had lived in relative peace and persecution suddenly broke out, Christians were far too willing to save their lives by worshiping the pagan gods and denying their faith. Christians were, therefore, in danger of growing complacent in their faith, of confusing their affirmation and acceptance by the social order with God's affirmation and acceptance. The possibility existed that Christians would come to order their lives, not according to the requirements of the gospel, but according to the expectations of the society that had finally accepted them. Extreme ease was a very real danger and one against which the leaders of the church needed to warn its members.

The opposite danger also existed: exclusivist rigorism. Some of the humble and faithful who had been members of the church in more difficult times resented the ease with which newcomers were admitted. Even more disturbing to some people was the fact that some of these newcomers, persons of prestige and power in society at large, were being allowed to transfer that power and prestige into their life in the church. In reaction, some people began insisting on a rigoristic form of Christianity whose hidden agenda was to exclude the arrogant newcomers.

This situation was clearly the case in North Africa, where the Donatist movement arose. In that part of the world the ancient Berber stock had been supplanted by people of Phoenician origin, and these people in turn had been conquered by the Romans. The result was a society in which Romans held the highest positions, followed by those people of Phoenician origin who had been absorbed into the Latin (Roman) culture, and on down to the Berbers who were usually relegated to the lowest echelons of society.

Before Constantine's conversion, Christianity had made significant inroads among the Berbers as well as among people of Phoenician stock. Those Latins who joined the church knew that by that very act they were identifying with an underclass in society and that the price could well be death—as was indeed the case with several of the leaders of North African Christianity. But after Constantine, things were different. The church was allied with the imperialistic oppressor.

To rescue the church from the control of such worldly hands, an insistence on the original purity and high cost of the faith was required. Many Christians felt that only the pure—those who had not wavered in time of persecution—had the true succession of the apostles. Out of such views and feelings a schism was born. The members of the rigorist party—the Donatists—refused to recognize the church that had made its peace with the Roman Empire. Eventually, a more militant branch of Donatism took to the hills and began practicing what amounted to guerrilla warfare. The Empire responded with military force, which only served to add fuel to the fire. Some of the more radical Donatists would eventually commit suicide rather than submit to what they regarded as the faithless church of the Empire. On one occasion several hundred Donatists jumped from a cliff in an act of mass suicide.

Anchorites and Fugitives

Other Christians who were equally convinced that the changes that were taking place were unhealthy for the church followed a different course of action. Instead of trying to set up a rival church against the one that was rapidly becoming a branch of the Empire, they simply fled from society (and, in a sense, from the church itself) in order to lead lives of austere discipline. This phenomenon was most notable in Egypt. Tens of thousands of people fled to the desert to live as *anchorites*, that is, as solitary hermits.

The word *anchorite* says much about the movement. *Anchorite* originally meant fugitive. Long before the advent of monasticism, hundreds of anchorites, or fugitives, lived in the Egyptian desert.

Recently discovered documents tell us a great deal about what life was like in Egypt under the Roman Empire. These documents clearly reveal that life was not easy for the people of the lower classes. Indeed, social structure in Egypt had changed little from the times of the pharaohs. A measure of social mobility was possible for people of Greek extraction; but most of the descendants of the ancient Egyptians, the Copts, were tied to a low social status. Those persons who were peasants practically belonged to the land. The people who practiced various crafts in small villages were subject to rigid and heavy systems of taxation. For peasants seeking a measure of freedom and for villagers who were unable to pay their taxes, the only recourse was flight to the desert. Therefore, even before the advent of Christianity the desert had been populated by anchorites.

The Roman oppression of Egypt had led to a great revolt against Emperor Diocletian in A.D. 295. At that time a vast current of conversion to Christianity was flowing among the Copts. Also of significance is the fact that in A.D. 303, Diocletian unleashed the worst persecution that Christianity had ever suffered. Since Christianity was not only illegal but also under persecution, many of the faithful, Coptic as well as

Greek, fled to the desert. They were simply following the example of the many Copts who had fled a few years earlier to escape Roman reprisal for the Egyptian revolt.

In the Egyptian desert Christian fugitives, or anchorites, joined earlier waves of people who had taken refuge there. So, we should not be surprised that monks were living in the desert prior to the conversion of Constantine.

However, not until Constantine's conversion did Christians flee to the desert en masse. Most of these people were no longer fleeing persecution. In fact, they were doing just the opposite. These new anchorites were fleeing security, ease, and the temptations they presented. Just as those persons who had fled earlier were making a statement, refusing to worship the gods, these new fugitives were also making a statement, refusing to accept the new, easy Christianity that many of them saw as little better than ancient paganism.

The most famous of the early monks of the Egyptian desert was Anthony. Although he is usually credited with being the founder of Christian monasticism, this view of him is an exaggeration. Other Christian "fugitives" were already in the desert when Anthony sought refuge there. In any case, what made Anthony famous was *Life of Saint Anthony*, written by Athanasius, the great bishop of Alexandria. This biography became one of the most popular books in the coming centuries and did much to shape the ideals of later monasticism.

According to Athanasius, Anthony was born of relatively wealthy parents in a village by the Nile. Anthony's parents died while he was still young, but his inheritance would have allowed him to live in moderate comfort for the rest of his life. However, when Anthony read the story of the rich young ruler and Jesus' call to "sell all that you have and distribute to the poor" (Luke 18:22b), he decided to follow this admonition. Anthony sold his possessions, gave the proceeds to the poor, and made certain that his sister was under the care and provision of the "widows" of the church. By this time not all who received the title *widow* were literally widowed women. That title also applied to other women who had decided to lead a life of celibacy and service to the church. Just as much as Anthony and the other anchorites of the desert, they were among the forerunners of Christian monasticism.

Having made these arrangements, Anthony withdrew to the desert. For many years he struggled there against all sorts of temptations. Finally a victor over these enemies, Anthony became famous for his wisdom and sanctity. His solitude was often interrupted by people who came to ask for his prayers, for his advice, or for his direction in the practice of the monastic life. After repeated efforts to hide from such distractions by fleeing farther into the desert, Anthony agreed that a number of monks could settle near him and that he would periodically share with them what he had learned over the years.

Since the *Life of Saint Anthony* was written years later and its author may have been quite busy with other matters when writing it, some people doubt the accuracy of many of its details. In any case, what is important is that Anthony, far from being the sole initiator of a movement that later grew, was one of the early examples of a movement that seems to have arisen spontaneously and then spread like wildfire. A few years after Anthony's death, travelers spoke, perhaps with a measure of exaggeration, of areas in the Egyptian desert that had become as thickly populated as cities. One such traveler spoke of a small area in Egypt where twenty thousand women and ten thousand men devoted themselves to the monastic life.

This life consisted of a discipline of renunciation combined with prayer and meditation. Renunciation involved poverty as well as celibacy. Monastics were supposed to have only what was absolutely necessary for living. Most of them frowned even on the possession of books. Therefore, they had to teach portions of Scripture to one another. They then memorized and repeated these Bible verses to themselves while weaving baskets, tending their garden, or doing other things. Renunciation also required that the monastics subsist on a very meager diet. On this point monastics often went to an extreme, as when they decided that a monk should eat seven olives (on the grounds that eating eight would be gluttony and eating only six would lead to pride).

This attitude reveals one of the directions the movement soon took: the direction of exaggeration and, in some cases, a craving for the spectacular. Some monastics roamed totally naked in the desert, their hair long and unkempt. They did so partly because they believed that the supreme act of humility was to act as if they were mad and thus not be admired for their holiness. Others, especially as the movement spread to Syria, would climb atop columns and remain there for years, even for the rest of their lives. These people were called *stylites*—from a Greek word meaning column. Sometimes two of these stylites, occupying adjacent columns but belonging to diverging theological factions, would spend years shouting insults at each other. Some of these people climbed trees. Members of one group walked on all fours, grazing like animals.

From Solitude to Community

Such exaggerations, however, should not detract from the movement as a whole, which represented a genuine and sincere attempt to live the Christian life more fully than seemed possible under the new conditions brought about by Constantine and his successors. Nevertheless, the life of absolute solitude left much to be desired, and its shortcomings soon gave rise to monastic communities. Some people simply were not strong enough to live alone year after year, seldom seeing anyone else. Furthermore, as we have seen in the case of Anthony, those who decided to become monks often sought out anchorites whom they would persuade to become their spiritual guides. Thus, loosely knit communities soon developed around many of the more famous monks. But the most powerful thrust toward communal monasticism came from the gospel itself, which clearly states that an important part of the Christian life is service to others—a service that is not possible when one lives in absolute solitude.

This new thrust may be seen in the life of Pachomius, who is usually credited with being the founder of communal monasticism (although, as was the case with Anthony, Pachomius was probably only one of many people who helped shape an entire movement). Pachomius was born in an Egyptian village. His parents were farmers of modest but sufficient means. He was a Copt (a native of Egypt descended from ancient Egyptian stock) and did not learn Greek until much later in his life. As a youth, he was drafted into the army. One day he was feeling miserable while stationed as a recruit in the city of Thebes when a group of Christians showed unusual kindness to him and his companions. Pachomius vowed that he would follow the example of these people and devote himself to the service of others.

For reasons that are not altogether clear, Pachomius was soon dismissed from the army. He immediately returned to his native area to learn about Christianity and to be baptized. Three years after his baptism he decided to become an anchorite and convinced a saintly monk to be his mentor. After seven more years of apprenticeship, he moved to a site some ten miles away. Pachomius lived there as a solitary until his brother John joined him.

This type of life, however, did not calm Pachomius's spirit. He was quite uneasy about whether he was doing the will of God and what that will was. In the midst of his anxiety he had a vision in which he was told that it was the will of God that he serve humans. He responded that he wished to serve God, not humans. But twice more the voice insisted that he was to serve God by serving others.

At this point in his life Pachomius decided to turn his home into a place where other people could find refuge and guidance in the monastic life. He and his brother began by building a larger enclosure and inviting others to join them. The first experiment was a failure. Pachomius's biographer said that this failure occurred because Pachomius did not at first insist on the very core of communal life: common property. His recruits insisted on their rights and privileges, on their ownership of various goods, and on not having to serve one another. After several years of heartbreak and constant struggle, Pachomius expelled all the recruits and decided to begin anew.

This second time around Pachomius insisted from the very beginning that any person who joined this community must renounce both private property and private will. He firmly believed that in order to have a truly common life, all members of the community must serve one another. Pachomius was convinced that people could not truly do so unless they held all things in common and were willing to renounce their own will in favor of absolute obedience. Pachomius himself, who held the position of supreme authority in the community until his death in 346, set the example. He constantly took on the most menial tasks and showed himself ready to confess his error when others proved him wrong.

Pachomius's sister Mary asked to join him. Instead of granting her request, he directed her to found a community for women near his own. During their lifetimes, Pachomius and Mary founded nine monasteries for men and three for women. All these communities were bound by obedience to Pachomius and to his successors. All the members of these communities gathered twice a year: at Easter to celebrate the Lord's Supper together and in the summer to discuss matters of administration.

Each of the Pachomian communities was patterned after an Egyptian village. The first thing a traveler would see was a high wall surrounding the entire community. The community had only one entrance, near which stood the building housing the gate-keepers. Two separate buildings were nearby. Male and female travelers were housed there. On this last detail Pachomius proved much more moderate than many monks whose fear and even hatred of women was marked. Even though the monks in Pachomian communities took vows of celibacy and were not permitted to engage in idle conversation with female guests, women were always welcome.

Farther into the compound most empty space was devoted to gardening, and there were a number of buildings for common use. Other structures were also present. The members of the community resided in these buildings in groupings based on the members' occupations. The common buildings included a church, where common prayer took place every morning and where a Communion service was held on Sundays. (On Saturdays the monastics all joined the people of a neighboring village for worship in the village church.) Other common buildings were the refectory (where the monastics gathered for their midday meal), a kitchen, a storehouse, and various workshops. The midday meal could include vegetables, fruit, bread, and even fish; but meat, wine, and oil were not permitted. Apparently the monastics also had a light evening meal which they ate in small groups in the various residential buildings. In the workshops as many of the needs of the community as possible were met. The monastics sold mats, baskets, and other goods they produced in order to be able to purchase things they needed but could not make themselves.

As stated above, the members of the community were housed in separate buildings according to their occupation. Besides buildings for the gatekeepers, there were also houses for weavers, bakers, cobblers, carpenters, and so forth, up to as many as forty different buildings in some communities. Each of these buildings had a cell for every two residents and a common room in which evening prayers were held as well as the evening meal.

11

The duties of the gatekeepers were varied. These people were responsible for the hospitality of the monastery. They were also responsible for meeting and questioning anyone who appeared at the gate asking for admission to the community. In such cases, postulants usually had to wait outside the gate for several days as a test of their resolve. When they were allowed into the compound, they lived with the gatekeepers while receiving basic instruction. After more time passed, postulants were allowed to join the community in prayer. Eventually a place was found for them in one of the residences, depending on the newcomers' occupations and talents.

Many of those who sought admission to the monastery were not Christians. They had to learn the rudiments of the faith and then receive baptism. Pachomius and his followers did not believe that the monastic life was a superior kind of Christian life, something that only mature Christians should attempt. On the contrary, they felt that life "in community," that is, in mutual service and holding all things in common, was a normal outcome of faith in Christ and baptism in his name. Therefore, they were willing to admit into their fellowship even those who had no experience of Christian life prior to coming to the monastery.

Still, the fact that pagans who had nothing but the slightest acquaintance with Christianity appeared at the gate of the monastery requesting admission is quite surprising. This fact points to what was said at the beginning of this chapter, that the desert was a place of refuge for many people who for various reasons decided to flee from society. Peasants and villagers who could not pay their taxes, slaves hiding from their masters, and young Copts seeking to avoid conscription into the hated Egyptian army found in the desert (often among Christian monks) a place of refuge. Pachomius himself ruled that his houses would not admit people who were not free to commit themselves to the monastic way of life. But ample evidence shows that other monastics did provide shelter for runaway slaves, tax evaders, and persons seeking to avoid military service.

On the other hand, not all who joined these communities were fleeing from social disadvantage. A number of people from the privileged Greek-speaking strata of society did join the Pachomian monasteries. As a result, bilingualism soon became a common practice in worship. Pachomius himself, in spite of his advanced age, learned Greek in order to be able to communicate with the Greek-speaking members of his community.

A Piety for Today?

People today have difficulty understanding the attraction that monasticism held for Anthony, Pachomius, and their contemporaries. Indeed, people are justified in rejecting various aspects of that form of piety—the manner in which many of the monastics punished and mistreated their bodies, their confusion of sex with sin, their legalism, and their excessive craving for solitude, among other things. But is that all we can say about their witness? Do these people not in some ways speak with a powerful voice to our generation, a generation in which once again it has become altogether too easy to call oneself a Christian?

Do they not stand as a word of judgment on our consumerism, in which we tend to measure ourselves by how much we consume rather than by Christian values? Do they not stand as a word of judgment on our egocentrism, in which we place ourselves and our own personal concerns above every other consideration? Do they not stand as a word of judgment on our wanton possessiveness, in which "mine" and "yours" are among the greatest obstacles to community? What, if anything, ought we to hear from these distant voices from the Egyptian wilderness, we who live in the wilderness of the twentieth century?

2

A Piety of Resistance

From Flight to Resistance

In a way, the piety of flight (discussed in the first chapter of this book) was also a means to resist the inroads that the new age was making on Christianity. The monastics of the desert felt that the best way to resist the temptations of pomp and power was to flee to the desert. Since their very act of refusing to live by the standards of the new age was an implied criticism of those standards, other people often considered them to be subversive. Furthermore, in some cases the monastics' actions did subvert the sociopolitical order by lending support to those who were seeking to flee from oppression. This fact was particularly apparent in the hospitality some monastics offered to runaway slaves and tax evaders, many of whom found refuge among the desert dwellers.

In order to avoid charges of hiding fugitives, Pachomius ruled that only those who were free to dispose of their own persons would be admitted into his communities. Later, legends developed of desert saints who were able to locate runaway slaves by miraculous means and who would direct their masters to them. The very fact that such rules and legends were necessary is an indication that at least some of the monastics did offer shelter to fugitives.

One such instance that is fairly well documented is the time when Athanasius, the bishop of Alexandria and one of the great figures of the fourth century, had to hide from the authorities. Bitter theological debates were raging. Athanasius defended the doctrine of the full divinity of Jesus Christ. For a number of reasons the emperor took the opposite view and ordered that Athanasius be arrested. At one point, Athanasius fled to the desert. For a number of years the monks hid him, apparently passing him on from one place to another as the imperial authorities approached. From his hiding places (and making use of monks as couriers), Athanasius continued corresponding with his supporters.

Athanasius himself, however, reflected a piety that was somewhat different from that of the monks of the desert. He wrote the famous *Life of Saint Anthony* and thereby contributed greatly to the spread of the monastic ideal. Athanasius was also deeply influenced by that ideal. However, he did not believe that his calling was to withdraw to the desert. He felt that his calling was to continue living in society and thus to engage in the difficult task of serving the Christian flock.

Athanasius was a deacon in the city of Alexandria when he traveled to Nicaea with Alexander, his bishop, in order to attend the great council that gathered there in 325. At that council one of the main issues discussed was the full divinity of the Son. The party of people who came to be known as *Arians* denied this concept. They argued that even though God had created the Son before the origin of time and space, the Son was a creature of the Father. However, the council declared that the Son was "of one substance with the Father" and not a creature. Henceforth, Athanasius devoted much of his time to defending this doctrine against the Arians.

The Arians soon gained political power, and Athanasius refused to bend before the imperial authorities. As a result, he spent much of his career in a series of exiles. Thus, he was one among many who established the validity of a piety of resistance—the same respectful resistance to the undue use of authority that had earlier cost the first Christian martyrs their lives.

As the fourth and fifth centuries progressed, imperial rulers began claiming increased jurisdiction in the life of the church. Church leaders insisted that all Christians, from the highest to the lowest, must live by Christian standards. When the imperial authorities did not do so or intervened too extensively in the life of the church, a number of these church leaders clashed with the emperors or with their representatives. While there were many such leaders, two in particular stand out: Basil the Great and Ambrose of Milan.

Basil the Great

Basil was born in Asia Minor into a family that had been Christian long before it became fashionable. Basil himself, however, was a fashionable young man. He studied at the best schools. Among his fellow students in Athens was one who would later become emperor—Julian, usually known as "the Apostate." Upon returning to his home town of Caesarea, Basil gave every evidence of being perfectly at home among the higher classes, to which he belonged both by reason of the wealth of his family and by reason of his own excellent education. His sister Macrina, who was the spiritual mainstay of the family, often rebuked him for being puffed up in a most unchristian manner. But Basil paid no attention until the sudden death of one of his brothers brought him to his senses.

At that point in his life Basil decided to withdraw from the world and to follow the monastic example. Macrina, whom he and his brother Gregory of Nyssa would later call "the Teacher," strongly supported his decision. At her prompting, Basil traveled to Egypt and to Syria, regions that were famous for their monasteries and teachers of asceticism, in order to learn about the monastic life.

By the time of his return to Caesarea, however, Basil was convinced that the life of strict solitude left much to be desired. Using the term *monastic* in its original sense of solitary, he declared that humans are not by nature solitary beings. He felt that human beings need to live in a community in order to be able to lead a life of love. If no one is near you, he would say, whose feet will you wash? The commandments of God require that we love both God and neighbor, and we cannot actively love our neighbor if we live without any neighbors.

Furthermore, Basil was convinced that the life that he and a small group of friends and relatives led was not a superior calling, something special for those Christians who wished to do more than was required of them, but was the life to which all Christians were called. True, many Christians lived for money, power, and prestige. But Basil did not believe that fact meant they should be expelled from the church. However, he thought that fact did mean that they had to be constantly called to the higher life of love and sharing.

When Basil became bishop of Caesarea, he made this concern one of the themes of his preaching. He made every effort to call his flock to a life more in accord with the principles of the gospel. In this context he would occasionally speak harsh words: "If someone who takes the clothes off another is called a thief, why should we give any other name to one who is able to clothe the naked, and does not do it?"[1] Or again, in a different context, "Beasts become fertile quickly, but they also cease being fertile quickly; but capital produces interest from the very beginning, and this continues to multiply endlessly. All that grows stops growing when it reaches its normal size; but the money of the greedy never stops growing."[2]

On these matters Basil was no rigid dogmatist. He was not saying that all Christians must sell everything they have or that private property must be abolished. Actually, there are indications that Basil retained some of his property throughout his entire life. What he meant—and apparently practiced to an astonishing degree—was that Christians must manage their possessions in a way that reflects their love of neighbor, not a desire simply to increase their wealth.

During Basil's time a "farm crisis" occurred in Asia Minor where he lived. Many of the small landowners were losing their property to rich magnates favored by imperial laws and edicts. Farmers who had been free landholders were being reduced to conditions of serfdom. Slavery, both explicit and implicit, was on the increase. While these events were taking place, those who made the unjust laws and those who profited from these laws called themselves Christians. Basil's understanding of Christianity, deeply influenced by the piety of the desert, by his sister Macrina, and above all by the teachings of Jesus, forced him to protest against such abuses. Thus, his piety, like that of Ambrose, led him to resistance against the customs and values of society.

Basil did not find himself practicing a piety of resistance only in regard to economic and social matters. In his time, a generation after Athanasius, the Arian controversy was still raging. Emperor Valens supported the Arian point of view and sought to impose his understanding of Christianity on his subjects. Basil, like Athanasius before him, defended the doctrine of Nicaea, that is, the full divinity of the Son.

On one occasion, when Valens planned a visit to Caesarea, he sent an envoy ahead to prepare the way. Apparently, part of that envoy's instructions was to obtain certain concessions from Basil, making it appear that the bishop agreed with the emperor's policies. The imperial legate was used to having his way, but Basil would not yield. The result was a stormy interview that ended with a heated exchange in which the legate threatened the bishop with seizure of his property, exile, torture, and even death. To this threat Basil is said to have responded, "All the goods in my possession which you could seize are these rags and a few books, to which you are welcome. As to exile, wherever I go I shall be God's guest. Torture? My body is already dead in Christ. And death would be a great boon, for it will take me to God more quickly."[3]

The legate declared that no one had ever dared to

speak to him in such a way. Basil responded, "Perhaps that is because you have never encountered a true bishop."[4] Basil was convinced that when the church was subservient to the emperor and his policies, its leaders were not true Christian pastors.

Ambrose of Milan

Ambrose, like Basil, was born into a family that was both wealthy and Christian. His father was a high officer of the Roman Empire. His headquarters were in the city of Trier (now in West Germany), where Ambrose was born. The young man soon gave proof of uncommon gifts, and his father made certain that he had the education that would best further a political career. In that career Ambrose was quite successful. He was a relatively young man when he became governor of Milan, one of the capital cities of the Empire.

In order to fulfill one of his responsibilities as governor, Ambrose decided to attend the election of a new bishop of Milan. Ambrose was a believing Christian, but he had not been baptized. (At that time many Christians felt that those who occupied official posts should postpone their baptism until their retirement, for it was likely that as imperial officers they would have to order the death penalty or otherwise incur major sin.) Because he had not been baptized, Ambrose was not technically a Christian. Therefore, he did not expect to participate in the election. His purpose in attending was simply to keep order, for the Christians in the city were bitterly divided between Arians and Nicenes (those who agreed with the decisions of the Council of Nicaea).

Ambrose was well aware that the election could lead to violence and riots. In order to prevent violence, Ambrose decided to use both his official authority and his ability as an orator. He addressed the crowd and called for calmness and moderation.

In the middle of his speech, however, he was interrupted by the cries of a child in the multitude: "Ambrose the bishop! Ambrose the bishop!" No one knows what the child meant. But apparently others took up the chant. The crowd was soon shouting, "Ambrose bishop! Ambrose bishop!"

Such an election was not part of Ambrose's plans for a career in imperial administration, and he refused to accept. When the people insisted, he tried to avoid becoming a bishop by every means at hand, including flight. But then came word from the emperor, who was delighted that one of his representatives was so popular. He ordered Ambrose to accept.

Ambrose realized that he had no choice and surrendered to the inevitable. Since he had not been baptized, he immediately received the holy rite. He was then quickly pushed through the various ranks of the hierarchy; and eight days after his baptism, he was consecrated as bishop of Milan.

Although Ambrose had not sought this position, he decided to perform his duties to the best of his abilities. He surrounded himself with able advisors. These people instructed him in theological and liturgical matters and also helped him with the many administrative and pastoral duties of the episcopate. By the time of his death, Ambrose was famous as a pastor, a theologian, and an able administrator. He was also instrumental in the conversion of Augustine, although he apparently did not realize how gifted his convert was.

What is most remarkable about Ambrose, however, is that the man who had planned a career as an imperial officer and who accepted the episcopate at the emperor's behest became most famous for his conflicts with imperial authorities and even with two emperors and an empress. Ambrose did not become involved in these conflicts because he wished to clash with his former masters. Ambrose simply felt that because he was a Christian and a bishop, he had to defend certain principles, even at the cost of arousing the ire of imperial rulers.

One of the first conflicts had to do with the death penalty. Emperor Gratian had decreed that a certain pagan was to die. Ambrose felt either that the penalty was too harsh or that the emperor had been misinformed and had acted unjustly. In any case,

Ambrose sought an interview with the emperor. He was not permitted to see the emperor, so Ambrose had no recourse but extreme measures. He somehow gained access to the field where Gratian was riding in a hunt, stood in front of Gratian's horse, and forced the emperor to listen to his plea. The courtiers were astounded and enraged. But Gratian acknowledged the justice of Ambrose's plea and withdrew the death decree that he had issued.

A second and more serious series of clashes took place with Empress Justina, who was regent for her young son. Justina was a convinced Arian. Ambrose was equally adamant in his support of the Nicene cause. When Justina ordered the bishop to surrender one of his churches so that Arian worship could be held in it, Ambrose flatly refused. A series of conflicts followed. Eventually, Ambrose and a multitude of his followers were besieged in a disputed church, surrounded by imperial troops who did not dare go in and take by force what the bishop refused to surrender. Inside the church Ambrose kept his followers' spirits up by composing hymns for all to sing. The resistance was too firm, and Justina was forced to withdraw the troops. But the conflicts continued until her son was murdered in a palace intrigue; and Theodosius, who already held part of the Empire, became sole emperor.

Theodosius was a supporter of the Nicene cause. Indeed, he convened the Council of Constantinople in A.D. 381, a council that practically put an end to the Arian controversy. Therefore, one could reasonably expect that Ambrose's conflicts with imperial authority would have ceased. However, such was not the case.

Ambrose clashed with imperial authority not only because it held a different theology than his but also because it held different values. Like Basil, he believed that the rich and the powerful have certain obligations to the weak and the poor. Furthermore, he declared that "nature intended for all things to be the common property of all, but what nature intended to be the property of all, greed and usurpation have made the property of a few."[5] He never hesitated to declare that those who held power or property owed a special responsibility to others.

On the basis of such principles Ambrose repeatedly questioned the policies of Theodosius—and questioned them to his face. Occasionally, Ambrose's zeal led him to support an unjust cause. For instance, when fanatical Christians in a small town burned the local synagogue, Ambrose argued before the emperor that they should not be forced to restore what they had destroyed because Christians ought not to be required to build a place of worship for unbelievers. At other times, however, Ambrose's resistance to imperial wishes was more appropriate.

On a certain occasion Theodosius had ordered that the population of Salonika (in Greece), where a riot had taken place, be massacred. A multitude of these people were attending games that the emperor was supposedly offering as a sign of forgiveness. These people suddenly found themselves surrounded by soldiers who killed everyone they could reach. The emperor's horrible edict had already been carried out when Ambrose learned of it. In response, Ambrose declared that the emperor would not be admitted to Communion until he repented of his sin and took steps to see that such a cruel act would not be repeated. Imperial officers threatened Ambrose, but he stood firm. Theodosius eventually acknowledged that the bishop was right and confessed his sin. Theodosius also ordered that henceforth a thirty-day waiting period would be required in all cases before a death penalty could be carried out.

A Piety for Today?

As we look at the lives of Athanasius, Basil, and Ambrose, some thoughts come to mind that are well worth pondering:

All these persons considered excessive wealth to be an impediment to faithful Christian ministry and even to faithful Christian obedience among the laity. Were they right?

Although they knew that they could not succeed at changing the entire structure of society, they nevertheless felt that it was their duty to measure that society by the standards of the gospel and to point out where society was found wanting. Were they justified in doing so, or were they mere idealistic dreamers?

Basil and Ambrose attained a measure of success. But they were willing to give it up in order to be faithful. Do we measure our discipleship by the standards of worldly success or by the standards of faithfulness?

All three were loyal Roman citizens. Yet, they eventually clashed with imperial authority. Although resistance and opposition to government was not their goal, their faith and their obedience to the gospel led them to such opposition and resistance. Can we think of contemporary situations in which Christians have been similarly led?

---

[1]From *Homily on Luke 12:16-21*, by Basil; Section 7.

[2]From *Homily on Luke 12:16-21*; Section 7.

[3]From *Ecclesiastical History*, by Sozomen; Book 6, Chapter 16.

[4]From *Ecclesiastical History*; Book 6, Chapter 16.

[5]From *On the Duties of Clergy*, by Ambrose; Book 1, Chapter 28, Paragraph 132.

3

A Piety of Order

The people we have studied in the first two chapters of this book—Anthony, Pachomius, Athanasius, Basil, and Ambrose—lived in times and places in which civil authorities were able to impose order. Occasionally, that order seemed to impede the full practice of the Christian life or to violate the principles of justice. In such situations the piety of Anthony and Pachomius led them to flee from society, but the piety of Basil and Ambrose led them to respond with protest and resistance. In all these cases, as well as in many their contemporaries faced, piety and justice clashed with civil order and authority.

Changing Times

There were, however, other times and circumstances. During Ambrose's lifetime serious disorders were occurring. Invasions of "barbarians" from beyond the borders of the Empire caused these disturbances. Ambrose himself was involved in providing help for refugees from those invasions and in raising money for the ransom of those whom the invaders held captive. In order to do so, he even sold the sacred vessels of Milan. When confronted with the accusation that this deed was sacrilege, he responded that God had appointed him to guard human vessels, not those made of gold or silver. Actually, the disorders of war did not directly reach Ambrose or the city of

Milan. The main difficulties Ambrose had were with emperors and other representatives of the civil order.

Shortly after Ambrose's death, however, the floodgates were open into the western part of the Empire. In 401, the invasions by the barbarians began in earnest. Throughout the vast Roman Empire, for decade after decade, people endured repeated devastation of their land, themselves, and their families at the hands of the barbarian invaders. Much of ancient civilization was destroyed. Barbarians captured the city of Carthage and established a kingdom that was noteworthy only for its cruelty. Not even Rome escaped the ravages of invasion.

Most people would find a long list of these invasions to be rather confusing. It is, and that is precisely the point. If we today would find this description confusing, imagine what it must have been like for those whose lot it was to live in Italy during those troubled times. A military invasion leaves nothing in its wake but misery, desolation, and pain. Without irrigation, an olive grove that an army destroyed for firewood took thirty to forty years to be restored to full production. While grain took only one year to be replanted and harvested, the working livestock had to be replenished before full production of grain could be resumed. This process took years. As to learning, who had the time to copy and preserve manuscripts when the entire area was being overrun by an invading army or when literacy itself was considered suspect by the conquerors? One can well understand how Christians living under such circumstances came to appreciate the value of order and predictability. In fact, one can understand that they might want to make order a high priority in their lives.

Benedict of Nursia

One such Christian was Benedict. He was born in the Italian town of Nursia, probably around 480. If so, he was nine or ten years old when the Ostrogoths invaded Italy and defeated Odovacar and the Heruli in a campaign that lasted four years, a bloody campaign that ended with the massacre of the last remaining Heruli troops. The Ostrogoths then took the spoils, assigning for themselves one third of all the land and its produce. Thus, during Benedict's early teens the news of war and its misery must have been fairly constant.

As Benedict grew older, the growing tensions and mistrust between the Ostrogroths and the native Italian population were quite apparent. He was in his mid-forties when the pope and others were executed by orders of King Theodoric. After Theodoric died in 526, his successors followed an even harsher policy. In 535, when Benedict was in his mid-fifties, the Byzantines invaded Italy; and refugees streamed from the wars in southern Italy. When he died, probably around 550, the Ostrogothic kingdom was struggling for survival. Thus, it is no accident that Benedict valued order, stability, and routine. Order, stability, and routine were luxuries that many in his time could not enjoy and whose lack seriously threatened the life of the church.

At first, Benedict simply sought to follow the same piety of flight that the early hermits practiced. He was about twenty years old when he withdrew to a cave in order to lead a life of staunch asceticism. There he faced temptations similar to those that had assailed Anthony in the desert and was able to overcome them only by punishing his body with extreme measures. Eventually, however, he decided that the purpose of the monastic life was not to destroy the body but to make it a more fitting instrument for God's work. Thus, from that time on he rejected the practices of extreme asceticism for which the hermits of the Egyptian desert had become famous.

A number of monks gradually gathered around Benedict. He sought to organize them in groups of twelve. But he soon found that these people were stubborn and egotistical and that they all wished to follow their own individual ways, coming and going as they pleased. One ancient document even says that they so resented Benedict's insistence on order and obedience that they tried to poison him. Whatever the case may have been, the fact is that Benedict eventually gave up on the lot of them and moved to Monte Cassino, a place so remote that a sacred grove still existed there where traditional pagan sacrifices were offered. In such inhospitable surroundings Benedict founded the monastery where he would remain for the rest of his life.

At Monte Cassino, Benedict gave his followers the *Rule*, his great contribution to Christian spirituality. The exact date of the *Rule* is not known, although tradition says Benedict gave it to his followers in 529. The *Rule* is a very short document but one that would have enormous impact in the Middle Ages and even to our day.

The *Rule* consists of seventy-three short chapters, the longest of which an average reader can read in five minutes. This document begins by declaring that there are four kinds of monks and that the *Rule* was written for only one of these four kinds. The other three kinds are (1) the anchorites (or hermits), of whom Benedict wrote nothing more; (2) those who live in groups of two or three without rule or master, doing whatever they please; (3) those whom Benedict called *gyrovagues*—a word of mixed Greek and Latin origin that can roughly be translated as gadabout.

Benedict's harsh words about the last two kinds of monks show two of the pillars on which his *Rule* stands: order and stability. The monks that he wished to lead were those who wanted to live a common life under a system of order and obedience and with a firm vow to remain in the community unless otherwise ordered by their superiors.

According to the *Rule*, these monks are to be under

the government of an *abbot*, a word that means father and therefore signifies both the authority of the abbot and the love and care with which he is to exercise his authority. In the rest of the *Rule*, Benedict repeatedly insists on the authority of the abbot. Therefore, in the second chapter, which deals with the abbot, he makes clear that the abbot is to be subject to the commandments of Christ, that he is to do everything out of love, and that he must be an example of humility. Also, the abbot must take care not to treat the highborn or those who come from wealthy families any differently than he does the rest of the monks.

The abbot has the final word. However, when matters of importance are to be decided, he is to consult with all the monks. On minor matters he is to seek the advice of the *elders* in the monastery—which does not necessarily mean those of greater chronological age but those with longer experience in the monastic life.

In the monastery the first rule is obedience. When a monk is commanded to do something, he must do it. He must do it, not with an unwilling obedience, but joyfully and as quickly as possible. If ordered to do something impossible, a monk should try to reason with his superior. However, if he is still commanded to do it, he must go and do his very best.

In order to foster this attitude of obedience and humility, no one in the monastery is to have any property. All things, including vestments, tools, and books, are the common property of the community, to be managed by the abbot. If a monk receives a gift from his family, he must give this gift to the abbot, to be used as the abbot sees fit.

This rule does not mean, however, that all monks will always receive the same. If any monk has extraordinary needs, the abbot will see that those needs are met. For instance, the *Rule* indicates that although the monks are usually not to have meat, those who are ill or elderly may be given meat as necessary. In any case, if a monk receives more than the rest, he must feel humbled that his need is greater.

Those who do not receive as much should be grateful that they do not need it.

The *Rule* states that all monks are to share in the work of the monastery. In particular, none but the infirm or those whose other work precludes it should be exempt from kitchen duties. These duties are to be assigned on a weekly basis, and the importance of this responsibility is to be acknowledged in that those appointed for such services each week are to be blessed in the chapel.

While self-indulgence was not permitted and silence was to be preferred over idle words, Benedict did not believe that much good would result from his monks subjecting themselves to extreme asceticism. At the two main meals two or even three dishes were served. Each monk also received a pound of bread a day and a measure of wine. The diet for children and the elderly, as well as for those who were sick, was more liberal, according to their needs. Also, if any monks were assigned to do work that was particularly strenuous, the abbot could order that they receive extra sustenance.

Thus, one of the most remarkable characteristics of the *Rule* is its flexibility. Benedict was well aware of differences in human nature and circumstances and made it quite clear that there was nothing wrong with taking such differences into account as long as no one used them as excuses for privilege or self-indulgence.

On the other hand, in the midst of a world in chaos, Benedict was also quite aware of the need for order and routine. Therefore, his *Rule* includes, besides matters such as those described above, detailed guidelines for the ordering of each day, including time for work and time for private and communal reading and prayers. Benedict was particularly interested in the periods of common prayer. He called for eight periods, or "hours," of prayer each day—not in the sense of sixty minutes each but in the sense of appointed times.

All Benedict's requirements reveal the practical bent of his mind. The body was not to be punished for the sake of punishment, although it was always to be kept under control as a tool fit for the service of God. Personal poverty was not an end in itself, a painful renunciation that one performed in self-punishment, but a means to an end. That end was community and obedience. So, although a monk could own nothing, the community could own whatever it needed in order to do its work. The *Rule* itself allowed for the exceptions that were certain to come about in the various matters it prescribed and thereby provided for its applicability in varying circumstances.

The Spread of the *Rule*

Benedict wrote his *Rule* primarily for his own monastery of Monte Cassino. His sister Scholastica organized a convent near Monte Cassino, where she also applied it. When Benedict died, probably around 550, only a handful of monasteries and convents in central Italy followed his *Rule*.

In 585, the Lombards destroyed Monte Cassino. The monks had to flee to Rome. This event, however, would prove fortunate for the spread of Benedict's *Rule*; for it was in Rome that Gregory the Great (pope from 590 to 604) became acquainted with the *Rule*. Partly through Gregory's influence, the *Rule*, or slight variations of it, began spreading to other parts of Europe.

For a while Benedict's *Rule* was in competition with almost three dozen other rules for monastic life. But by the ninth century it was simply known as "the Rule" and had practically supplanted every other rule in the vast Carolingian Empire. By the twelfth century Benedict's *Rule* was followed all over Western Europe, as far east as Poland; and the crusaders had taken it to Palestine. A convent of Benedictine nuns even lived in Greenland. After that time most monks and nuns in Western Europe were Benedictines. Also, even those who belonged to various orders, some of them with their own rules, owed much to the inspiration of Benedict and his *Rule*.

Benedict's *Rule* did not only influence monastics. Many people among the clergy and the laity followed the "Liturgy of the Hours," or "Holy Office," as his program of prayer and devotion came to be called. The members of the higher classes, who were more literate than most people and who had the necessary leisure, often owned a "Book of Hours," or "Breviary," which they read either in private or in household devotions. Since many of the poorer peasants lived on land the monasteries or the church owned, their lives too were regulated by the "Hours, " which they followed at a distance. Thus, Benedict and his *Rule* became both the soul and the clock of Western Europe.

Furthermore, the monasteries where the *Rule* was observed also served as schools for children, hostelries for travelers, hospitals for the sick, pharmacies for entire communities, and so forth. Indeed, the Benedictine monastery, probably even more than the papacy, was at the very heart of medieval Christianity as the common people experienced it. The Benedictine monastery was also the most stable economic entity during the early centuries of the Middle Ages.

A Piety for Today?

When we look at Benedict's piety, we find much in it that is familiar to us and much that is foreign. We are probably quite comfortable with his call for moderation and flexibility. Indeed, having moved from the exaggerations of the desert hermits to Benedict's moderation, we are relieved. Most of us have little use for unkempt saints. Therefore, we can readily understand why Benedict rejected the extreme forms of asceticism that the desert hermits exemplified. His reasons, however, were deeply theological. He was not simply trying to avoid exaggeration, as any sensible person would do. He was convinced that the body is a creature of God, created to be God's instrument. One must control and train it, but one must not punish it to the point that some of its usefulness to God is lost. This point of view accounts

31

for both Benedict's moderation and for his insistence on a set routine of prayer and devotion.

Most of us have a daily routine and can see its value. While the practice of a routine of prayer and devotion has fallen into relative disuse in our society, all sorts of other routines exist that are similar to what Benedict proposed. Many of us are exercise buffs. We know that in order to get the required exercise, we must develop a routine that we follow regularly, even when we do not feel like doing so. Other people are accustomed to having regular hours of work and feel somewhat at a loss when vacations or retirement break that routine. Therefore, in theory at least, we can see the value of a prescribed time set aside for prayer and devotions.

However, for many of us that practice is little more than a theory. At best, we feel that eleven o'clock Sunday morning is the "sacred hour" and that we ought to say grace before meals. Beyond that, few of us have a disciplined program of prayer and devotions. Furthermore, many of us feel that such a discipline would be too rigid or legalistic and that our prayer under such conditions would lose much of its spontaneity. But the truth is that when our prayer life lacks structure, it suffers and almost disappears.

Thus, as we look at Benedictine piety and order, a piety expressed in orderliness, we may be forced to admit that, foreign as it may seem to us, there is much to be said for the life of prayer and devotion that Benedict's *Rule* fosters.

We also need to think about the entire question of obedience. Obedience is something we moderns find difficult to understand or appreciate. We have been taught to trust our own feelings and understanding and not to surrender our freedom and responsibility. Therefore, when we read Benedict's words on obedience and humility, we are likely to find them totally unacceptable. In so doing, perhaps we are right. What we must remember, however, is that Benedict's view of obedience was set in the context of a life of community. In a community where all share in everything, material goods as well as goals in life, the sort of obedience that the *Rule* advocates is probably not as out of place as it seems to us today who live in a society that rarely provides even a sense of community.

Finally, we need to think about Benedict's insistence on stability, or, perhaps more precisely, "stayability." Benedictine monks and nuns were expected to spend their entire lives in the same monastery unless they were ordered to move for some specific reason. Benedict proposed this rule in a society where chaos reigned, where people constantly had to move, and where, therefore, people had a deep longing for roots. He did not propose that everyone stay where they were born. Indeed, the distance from Nursia, where Benedict was born, to Monte Cassino, where he died, is great. What Benedict proposed was that once people found a community that they wanted to call their own, they should make a commitment to it for the rest of life.

In a mobile society such as ours, most of us are ambivalent about stability and mobility. While we value our mobility (and many of us are willing to move in order to advance our careers), we also long for roots, for a permanent community where we can establish long-term relationships. Those who study trends in our society are finding that more and more people are saying that "roots" and stability are more important than mobility, either geographic or social. In fact, many pastors report that they have church members who refuse to move because they value the Christian community of their church. In many ways this attitude is not so far removed from Benedict's views on stability.

Quite clearly, we cannot apply Benedict's *Rule* directly to our situation today. Nevertheless, there is much in the piety behind that *Rule* from which we can learn and profit.

4

A Piety of Poverty

Changing Times

Around the year 1050, changes began taking place that would alter the face of Western Europe. These changes were subtle. Historians can now point to them and analyze them because we look at them with a perspective of centuries. For those who lived at the time, things were not as clear. A general uneasiness was in the air, and people wondered and thundered at many of the things they saw happening around them. However, long-term trends and their interconnectedness are not easy to see when one is submerged in them.

First of all, an agricultural revolution was taking place. New and more efficient harnesses for horses enabled deeper and faster plowing. This advance led to the development of a better plow. Also, techniques such as crop rotation and fertilization of soils increased yields. Windmills also became common a few years later.

As commerce grew, specific geographical areas that were better suited for a particular type of crop became increasingly specialized in that crop. As a result, the total yield of the land increased.

Such increased productivity meant that the land was able to sustain a larger population without a proportional increase in the labor required. Thus, a larger population began to develop. At first, most of this population moved to new lands, clearing them for agricultural production. But this movement in turn produced larger agricultural surpluses, which resulted in further population growth.

Although a quite promising agricultural revolution was at the heart of these changes, these changes did not always lead to better living conditions for the masses. Greater agricultural yields meant the possibility of more soldiers for larger armies and more constant warfare among feudal lords, who in this new era could be less concerned about supplying their households. Also, since peasants could produce more, their taxes were increased. As a result, a poor crop would be even more disastrous than before; that is, peasants would still have high taxes but fewer resources to pay them. Thus, while Europe as a whole was going through a period of prosperity, that prosperity on the larger scale often turned into chaos and misery at the local level.

While some members of the growing rural population went on crusade (see *The Crusades: Piety Misguided*, another book in this series), others settled in nearby towns. The growth of towns, along with increasing specialization in various fields of agricultural production, gave rise to a commercial revolution. Before this time trade had taken place almost exclusively at the local level. Long-distance trade was limited to luxury items. In terms of primary needs, each village was self-sufficient or nearly so. But in this new age a village that had come to specialize in producing wine had to trade for its food, and one that produced cereals had to trade for its wine.

What was true of villages was even truer of the rapidly growing towns. The surrounding fields were not sufficient to feed urban populations. Nearly one hundred thousand people came to be concentrated in cities such as Milan and Venice. In order to survive, a city had to live by trade. Merchants, until then considered inferior parasites who produced nothing and lived off the work of other people, became increasingly necessary and powerful. By the end of the Middle Ages, they were a highly respected and important part of society.

The commercial revolution, with its long-distance trade, required an easy means of exchange and led to the reintroduction of money. Castile (in Spain) was the first regional kingdom to mint a gold coin. It did so in 1175. In 1202, Venice employed some of the silver it received from the leaders of the Fourth Crusade to mint a larger coin, worth twenty-four pennies. Soon the other major cities of Italy followed suit; so did France and England.

While money made commercial transactions easier, it was also dangerous to transport. Money could easily be lost or stolen. Thus arose the system of letters of credit of which our modern credit systems are an heir. Full-time bankers—also a new creation of the age—could make money available to merchants in distant places without actually moving large amounts of gold or silver.

The impact of these changes was not always welcome. While new methods of finance, growth of cities, and long-distance trade did in fact increase the wealth of Europe, they also produced dislocation, confusion, and suffering.

Commerce did not always result in better living conditions for all people. The increased wealth of the rich did not necessarily trickle down to the poor. On the contrary, the very impersonality of money enabled the rich to ignore the poor to a degree that was difficult in earlier times. The growth of cities, where the ancient feudal system no longer held, meant that no one felt responsible for the urban poor. Earlier, many a feudal lord, while exploiting his peasants, at least felt that utter destitution and hunger in his domains would speak ill of him. So, he sought to alleviate bad conditions, at least to a certain degree. However, in the new era city merchants could tell themselves that the fact that some people were starving in the city was neither their fault nor their responsibility. At best, they felt obligated to give alms.

A Changing Piety

The new age also brought a piety with a different emphasis. During the early Middle Ages, religious thinkers usually asserted that the root of all sin was pride. But in the new era greed began competing with pride for that dubious honor. The piety of Benedict and his followers was particularly directed against pride. His concern about the harmful effect of pride was the reason for Benedict's insistence on humility and obedience. Benedict and his followers during the earlier Middle Ages refused to own personal property, not because they thought voluntary poverty was particularly virtuous, but because they believed that owning personal property fostered pride. In the new era many people felt that money itself was evil and that poverty, when one embraced it voluntarily out of love for God, was a virtue. The poverty of Jesus became a theme of many a sermon and devotional writing. Since Jesus was poor and did not even have a place to lay his head, one way to imitate him was to embrace a life of voluntary poverty.

The popularity of the ancient legend of Saint Alexis reflected the widespread acceptance of this point of view. In the eleventh century this legend was embellished and made the object of a long epic poem. According to this legend, Alexis was the son of a Roman patrician. On the day of his marriage to an equally wealthy bride, Alexis left his home in order to pursue the monastic life. After several years he returned to his own home, but his ascetic practices had changed his appearance so much that no one recognized him. He then lived for seventeen years in a corner under the steps of his house. When Alexis died, those who should have been his servants prepared to bury him. At that time some papers he still carried gave away his identity.

The story of Alexis moved Peter Waldo, a merchant from Lyons, to embrace a life of poverty. Significantly, he made preaching part of his way of life, calling others to repentance and to a similar life of poverty. Soon a band of followers gathered around him. When the archbishop of Lyons ordered them to cease preaching, they appealed to the pope. In Rome, they did not fare much better. Trapped in theological subtleties and then mocked by those appointed to examine them, Waldo and his followers returned to Lyons with no more than permission to continue living in poverty and to preach only if their archbishop would allow it. When they realized that the archbishop would never change his mind, they decided to preach anyway. Officially declared to be heretics in 1184, the Waldensians, as they were called, suffered many martyrdoms. Those who survived hid in secluded valleys in the Alps.

The Waldensians were just one of the many movements that arose in those perplexing times. Adherents insisted on voluntary poverty as a response to the greed that appeared to rule the world and the church. The members of most of these groups were generally orthodox, believing essentially what other Christians believed. However, other groups existed that were more clearly heretical, holding doctrines far removed from traditional Christian belief. Such was the case of the Albigensians. Their appeal was greatly due to their austere life, the poverty of their leaders, and the marked contrast between their lifestyle and the opulence of many a bishop.

Francis of Assisi

Of all these movements, the most important by far was that of the Franciscans. Francis, whose real name was Giovanni, grew up in the town of Assisi. He got the nickname *Francesco* for reasons that scholars still debate. One explanation is that because his mother was French, he loved and sang the songs of French troubadours. Another explanation is that his father insisted that he learn French so that he could be a successful merchant. In any case, Giovanni ennobled his nickname to the point of making it one of the most cherished names in Christendom.

Francis's father was a successful cloth merchant. He was so successful that he entertained dreams of opening the way for his son to become a knight and thus enter the ranks of the minor nobility. In those changing times, being a merchant was both a source of power and a source of shame. Pietro di Bernardone, Francis's father, lived in that ambiguity. He therefore dreamed for young Giovanni his fondest dream, that some day he would be made a knight.

For a while young Francis tried to fulfill his father's fantasy. He even joined the military force that the town of Assisi sent against the rival city of Perugia. He ended up a prisoner in Perugia for over a year. After Francis's release through the payment of ransom, his father had him fitted in an expensive and showy suit of armor and sent him off on the Fourth Crusade. Francis had hardly left, however, when he was moved to compassion by a ruined knight, lacking armor. Francis gave the man much of his equipment. A few days later, Francis sold the rest and returned home to face an irate father who repeatedly reminded him that he had paid the price of a farm for his son's military equipment. His father shouted, "Where is my money? My money?!"

For quite some time, Francis was simply a young man about town. He spent as little time as possible in his father's cloth business and enjoyed great popularity among his peers. Much of that popularity probably had to do with the liberality and carelessness with which he spent his father's money. But his popularity was also based on his magnetic personality and on his appreciation for beauty, which he could find as readily in a troubadour's song as in a young woman or in a flower by the roadside.

For a long time, however, the apparently carefree young man had been struggling with himself and with God. Perhaps at the heart of that struggle was an ambivalence about money and glory. In any case, one day in the midst of drunken revelry, his friends noticed that Francis was strangely silent. When they finally caught his attention and asked him what was the matter, he responded that he had decided to wed "the fairest, the noblest, the richest lady of all." They laughed at his conceit and continued their carousing. But he meant that he had decided to embrace a life of poverty or, as he put it, to marry "Lady Poverty."

Then followed a series of episodes that tested his character and conviction. His father could not understand what was happening to Francis. The shouts of "my money" became more strident as Francis now spent what he was given, no longer in feasting, but in giving to the poor. Finally, the great confrontation took place. In the public square in front of the great church, Francis's father dragged him before the bishop to demand that Francis either behave or renounce his rights as heir. Before the astonished crowd of onlookers, Francis stripped himself of every item of clothing, placing it all at his father's feet. Then he declared out loud, for all to hear, "From this day on I can truly say 'Our Father, which art in heaven,' for Pietro di Bernardone is no longer my father . . . . Naked I go to meet my Lord."

As his father picked up the discarded garments—and a purse of money that Francis had also returned to him—the bishop covered Francis with his cloak. Francis was twenty-three years old.

Dressed in a gardener's rags, Francis then withdrew to the forest. He intended to live there as a hermit and to rebuild a small chapel that was in disrepair. But after spending some time in solitude, he was moved by the reading of Matthew 10:5-10, which describes Jesus sending his disciples on a mission and telling them to carry no purse. Francis felt this passage of Scripture was a direct commission from the Lord. He believed he was to live in poverty, as he was already doing. However, Francis realized the purpose of this life was not to live as a hermit in solitude but rather to be free to preach wherever people gathered, that is, mainly in the cities.

Thus began the Franciscan movement. Francis gathered a small band of followers and then went to Rome to request papal approval for his mission. The pope was Innocent III, the most powerful man ever to occupy that post. The contrast between this haughty Roman aristocrat and the humble *poverello*—little poor one—from Assisi must have been astounding. But the two men understood each other, and Francis was able to leave Rome with the pope's blessing.

From that point on, the movement grew by leaps and bounds. Many of those who first joined were sons of merchants, like Francis himself. Some were from the nobility. Others were of humbler station. A woman named Clare founded a parallel order for women. She had been impressed by Francis's devotion to poverty from the very beginning.

The movement was essentially one of laypersons, for Francis was never ordained. (The same was true much earlier of Benedict and most of his followers.) Soon there were hundreds of "little brothers,"—friars minor—as they called themselves. Then there were thousands. Many people thought the Franciscans were mad. Others thought that their carefree life was an affront to those who worked for a living. As is often the case, those who most criticized the Franciscans for not working were members of the higher classes who themselves did not have to work very hard. Many of the poor were astonished at these people who willingly and joyously decided to be poor when they could live in comfort. Among the church hierarchy, many admired and supported the movement. The Franciscans represented a valuable alternative to various heretical movements. However, other religious leaders declared that Francis and his followers were too idealistic, that they undercut the life of the church by tacitly criticizing those clerics who did not live in poverty.

Francis died in 1226. A few years later the movement had penetrated the most prestigious universities in Europe, some of whose professors embraced it. However, some professors resented the implicit criticism by their colleagues who vowed to live in voluntary poverty. The University of Paris was embroiled in a long and bitter controversy among its professors as to whether Jesus Christ called people to the life of poverty.

Francis himself was aware of the difficulties that lay ahead for the movement. He knew that his ideal of voluntary poverty was difficult to sustain. In his will Francis expressed his wishes for the order he had founded. He wanted to make certain that his followers never abandoned the ideal of voluntary poverty. After his death, however, his followers were divided. Some held to strict obedience to Francis's will. Others agreed with the pope. He said that the will was not binding and that while each friar was to be poor, the order itself could hold property. The controversies that ensued do not concern us here. What is important is that, for whatever reasons, the issues of property, money, and voluntary poverty gripped the minds and souls of the people of the thirteenth century precisely at the time when the foundations for modern capitalism were being laid.

A Piety for Today?

Two elements in Franciscanism are worth pondering: its connection with the growth of cities and its emphasis on preaching. The structure of the church at that time, divided into geographic parishes, was unable to cope with the mobile society of the thirteenth century. Also, the ancient piety of Benedict and the older monastics, with its emphasis on silence and its distrust of words, was sadly out of place in the urban setting, which is above all a verbal setting. In a way, Franciscanism and its wandering preachers met the needs that the changing circumstances created. The success of the movement was due not only to

Francis's sincerity and singleness of heart but also to the way in which he and his followers responded to those circumstances. What are the changing circumstances of our day? What are the structures in church life that best respond to them in faithfulness to the gospel?

As we seek to respond to such questions, we must also ask, Does Francis's message and practice of poverty have something to teach us today? When most of us think of Francis, we think of birds resting on his shoulders, of the legends of the taming of "brother wolf," and of his hymn of joy in creation. We do not think of what to him was the necessary requirement and foundation for a life of overpowering love, namely, his betrothal and marriage to "Lady Poverty."

Francis was the gentle and loving person that we see depicted in garden statues. But when it came to money, he could be harsh and inflexible. When a brother touched a coin, even though it was only to throw it away, Francis ordered that he take it with his lips and bury it in a dunghill. Was Francis's attitude about money just a pathological phobia that resulted from his conflicts with his father? Or was it, as he firmly believed, the very basis for the life of self-giving love that he and his friars were to live? This is much more than an idle question or one of mere historical significance. If Francis was right, it means that an irreconcilable contradiction exists between the longing for love and peace that we express when we place a statue of Francis by a fountain and our unquenchable thirst for more money and more possessions. Can we really learn from Francis without undergoing in our own way a clash with our own Pietros di Bernadone who are always shouting, "Money, my money"? Can we really learn from Francis without challenging the economic injustices of our time and our own participation in them?

5

A Piety of Reformation

As we move from Francis of Assisi in the thirteenth century to Catherine of Siena in the fourteenth, we find radically changed circumstances. Innocent III, the pope with whom Francis met in Rome, was the most powerful and prestigious pope in history. By contrast, Catherine lived at a time when the papacy had lost much of its former glory.

Catherine of Siena

Catherine was born in 1347 in Siena, a city in central Italy (about forty miles south of Florence). She was the twenty-fourth of twenty-five children of a dyer of wool and his wife. The twenty-third was her twin sister, who did not survive.

From a very early age Catherine attended the nearby church of San Domenico, where there was also a monastery. Dominic, a contemporary of Francis, had founded the Order of Preachers, usually known as *Dominicans*. They followed vows of poverty similar to those of the Franciscans but with more emphasis on learning and theological studies. Like the Franciscans, the Dominicans had, besides a "second order" for women, a "third order," or tertiaries, who followed much of the lifestyle of the order but without actually joining a convent or monastery.

Catherine wished to become a Dominican nun. Her mother, who was hoping to see her married to a wealthy merchant, objected. Eventually, when she was eighteen, Catherine was allowed to become a Dominican tertiary. As such, she participated more fully in the life of San Domenico.

Catherine learned how to read so she could participate with the Dominicans in the hours of prayer that were a common feature of monastic life. Indeed, a vast portion of the Scripture and theology that she knew she learned by participating in such communal prayer. Also, Catherine soon gathered around her a number of companions who were both her disciples and her teachers. They marveled at the wisdom of her words and she gained most of her knowledge from them.

Even as a child, Catherine had visions. One of the experiences she cherished was the "mystical marriage with Christ," in which Jesus Christ came to her, married her, and gave her a ring that only she could see but which always reminded her of the One to whom she belonged. Later in life she spent four hours during which she appeared to be dead. When she recovered, she declared that she had seen the glory of the redeemed and the pain of the damned. Catherine therefore redoubled her efforts for the salvation of humankind.

As a mystic, all that she wished was to be alone with her heavenly bridegroom. Then, she had an unexpected experience, which she later described to her confessor and biographer, Raymond of Capua. According to Raymond, it all began when the Lord told Catherine to leave her prayers and join her family at dinner. She objected, feeling that she was being sent away from the religious life. She asked the Lord to keep her with him. To this request Christ replied,

"It is not my purpose to separate you from me, but rather to bind you even closer to me by the bond of your love to your neighbor. . . . Remember that when you were young you dreamed of dressing like a man in Dominican attire and going abroad to save souls."

"How can this be done? " she asked like Mary before her.

"As I in my goodness shall plan and arrange, " replied the Lord.

"How can I, who am nobody, do any good for souls?" objected Catherine. "You know that my sex stands in the way. People have no place for women to do all this, and it is improper for women to go about with men."

"Who but I created humankind? I made them male and female. Who but I can determine where my grace will be poured? Before me there is neither male nor female, nor distinction of classes. . . . Now human pride has surpassed all limits, especially the pride of those men who think that they are wise and learned. I can no longer withhold my justice, to put them back where they belong."[1]

After experiencing that vision, which took place when she was twenty-one, Catherine was less reluctant to participate in the common life of her family. She also became more involved with the poor and the sick in Siena. At that time her reputation as a worker of miracles began spreading. Eventually, people hoping for a miracle would come to her from long distances. Others just wanted a word with her.

As Catherine become more involved in the community around her, she became aware that much more than the poor and the sick in Siena was wounding her Lord's heart. War ravaged the entire countryside as city fought against city and conspiracy followed conspiracy. Bands of mercenaries, many of them unemployed and simply living off the land, destroyed life and property. She wrote a passionate letter to them—or rather, she dictated it. At that time Catherine could read but not write, and there is some doubt that she was ever able to write. She called on the mercenaries to stop ravaging the land and either put aside their arms or use them in a holy crusade against the infidel. Although the Crusades had run their course, many people in Western Europe still longed for the return of those days that seemed so glorious. Catherine was among them. She repeatedly issued a call for a new crusade as a remedy for the constant warfare in Europe in general and in Italy in particular.

Letters, however, were not enough for Catherine. She traveled to Florence in 1374 and attended the Dominican General Chapter. She gained the admiration of those present and persuaded many to follow her way. While there, she met Raymond of Capua (referred to earlier in this chapter), a Dominican who later became an outstanding leader of that order, thanks to her influence.

When she returned to Siena, Catherine found that the plague was ravaging the city and that those who were not ill were trying to hide from the disease or had abandoned the city altogether. Catherine, her friends, and Raymond of Capua took on the task of caring for the sick.

The next year Catherine traveled to Pisa. She tried to persuade the leaders of that city and its allies to abandon a league that had been formed in opposition to the pope, a league that was preparing for war. Again she called for a holy crusade. This effort was the first of Catherine's many attempts to promote peace. War, she felt, should be avoided at all costs. She criticized not only the pope's adversaries but also the pope himself for having resorted to arms.

In 1376, the Florentines called on her to intercede for them before the pope, who had placed them in interdict, that is, had forbidden that the sacraments be administered within the bounds of their city-state. She agreed to go to Avignon to represent the Florentines, who in turn promised to accept whatever conditions for peace she could negotiate with the pope. (During this time the pope did not live in Rome but in the papal city of Avignon, on the southeastern border of France.) Catherine did not know it at the time, but she later discovered that the Florentines were using her. They had also sent another representative, with different instructions, to Avignon.

Catherine knew how to be harsh, and her letter to the Florentines thundered against their treachery and impiety. However, she did not give up on her struggle for peace. In 1378, she found herself once again in Florence, this time at the pope's request, pleading for peace. Once again the Florentines used her according to their convenience. Once again Catherine fumed, let her anger be known, and continued her work for peace.

One of Catherine's most cherished dreams did come true. For years she had been pleading with the pope to return to Rome. Gregory XI had repeatedly declared that he was willing to do so but that conditions in Italy were not safe. Catherine, of course, had done everything she could to bring about peace; but she also sent a letter to Gregory urging him to have faith and come to Rome: "Be a true successor of St. Gregory: love God, and not your relatives, friends or material needs. . . . Put an end to these ills, and act as a Christian. Forward to the completion of what you have started! The Devil is using all his wiles to hinder your march; but do not delay, for your delay has caused many evils. . . . Vicar of Jesus, you must sit on your throne again."[2]

This is a remarkable letter from an unlearned laywoman to the man whom she respectfully and sincerely called "Vicar of Jesus." In telling him to love God rather than his relatives, she was condemning the nepotism (favoritism granted to relatives or close friends) that was rampant in Avignon and which the pope himself practiced. She even dared to tell the pope that he was resisting the will of God. Yet, she said all this in a most respectful tone.

Historians disagree on the extent to which Catherine's insistence was instrumental in convincing

Gregory that the time had come to return to Rome. In any case, whatever the pope may have thought of her letters, the pressure of public opinion that Catherine had helped create did much to end the so-called "Babylonian captivity" at Avignon.

However, Catherine's dream had hardly been realized when it turned into a nightmare. Gregory brought an army with him from Avignon. A few weeks after his arrival, these troops clashed with the Italian populace in a riot that left over four thousand people dead. Gregory tried to calm these "troubled waters"; but he was already considering a move back to Avignon when he died, only a few months after returning to Rome.

The cardinals who had to elect Gregory's successor had been named while the papacy was in Avignon. Most of them were French. Therefore, the people of Rome feared that the cardinals would either elect a pope who was willing to return to Avignon or that the cardinals would flee before the election, go to Avignon, and there elect Gregory's successor. A riot occurred, and the cardinals were forced to proceed to an election immediately. Their choice was an Italian of austere life and profound religiosity who took the name *Urban VI*.

Urban VI set out to correct the ills that had plagued the church for several generations. Even a wiser man than Urban would have found this task quite difficult. Most of the people around the pope, including the cardinals, had become wealthy on the basis of the corrupt practices that the new pope condemned. When Urban's reforming decrees met with resistance among the cardinals, he accused them of being not only corrupt but also traitors. Soon the word spread that the pope was mad. Whether this charge was true or not, Urban was obviously quite unwise and made more enemies than was necessary.

The cardinals began deserting him, first the French and then some of the Italians. Urban simply appointed twenty-seven new cardinals from among his supporters. The dissident cardinals, by now a majority of those who had elected Urban, gathered at Anagni. Under the protection of the king of France, they declared that Urban's election had taken place under duress and was therefore null and void. They then proceeded to elect a new pope. Their choice took the name *Clement VII* and set up his residence at Avignon.

As a result, two popes and two Colleges of Cardinals were in existence. This disastrous state of affairs, called the Great Western Schism, would last from 1378 to 1423. During all that time there would be at least two rival popes. At times there would be three. Since the Hundred Years' War was still in progress, each nation chose the pope it would acknowledge on the basis of its political allegiance. France and her allies supported the popes in Avignon. England and her allies were for those in Rome.

Catherine had only three more years to live when the schism began. She devoted those years to promoting the cause of Urban VI, whom she considered to be the legitimate pope. However, her support of Urban did not mean that she excused his excesses. On the contrary, while staunchly supporting his cause, she wrote to him telling him in no uncertain terms that he had brought his difficulties on himself by his lack of tact and by his lack of Christian love. Her hope was that a great council would be called to settle the matter and end the schism—a hope that did not become a reality until many years after her death. Meanwhile, she insisted that, in spite of all his faults, there could be only one pope, the one in Rome.

Feeling at a loss in the midst of so many enemies and difficulties, Urban summoned Catherine to Rome. There she spent the last years of her life, meeting with the pope and with the cardinals. She offered them her advice and composed letters to promote the peace of the church. Catherine died on April 29, 1380, when she was thirty-three years old.

Catherine left behind a writing that she simply called "my book" but is commonly known as the *Dialogue*. Some of her biographers claim that as she approached the task of writing this book, she miraculously learned how to write. Others say that she dictated it. In any case, the *Dialogue* is cast in the form of a conversation between God and Catherine. This approach is a common device in mystical literature. What is significant about the *Dialogue*, however, is that it is a mystical work on the reformation of the church. The book deals not only with the soul's relation with God but also with the ills affecting the church and how they are to be attacked.

Thus, in the midst of this work of mystical conversation, God breaks forth in harsh condemnation of those who seek to make money as ministers of the gospel: "You want your followers to buy themselves all over again when they come for what you have received as a gift. . . . You are like a thief, deserving eternal death, for you have robbed the poor."[3] Then God goes on to comment on the basis on which ministers are chosen: "They only look to their social standing, their appearance and their wealth, their ability to speak much and very eloquently. And even worse, someone will comment on their good looks!"[4] In this book God also says that there are those in the ministry who pay more attention to their horses than to souls and that this is fitting, for they themselves have become beasts!

Such harsh words did not go unnoticed. Although Catherine now has many admirers, during her lifetime she had many enemies. They repeatedly sought to discredit her. They even tried to have her declared a heretic and condemned. Many mystic visionaries who, like Catherine, ran afoul of powerful interests met that fate. Her enemies were not able to succeed, however, not only because of her fame but also because she had learned much theology from her group of learned friends. These people had gathered around her to listen to her wisdom, but she had also learned much from them. Thus, in spite of being almost illiterate, Catherine's theology was impeccable. Those who sought to trap her in theological subtleties did not find doing so an easy task.

Catherine was declared a saint in 1461. In 1970,

Pope Paul VI added her name, and that of Teresa, to the list of "Doctors of the Church," an honor previously granted to only thirty men and to no women.

A Piety for Today?

Two things about Catherine seem surprising to most contemporary readers. The first of these is the respect and attention that an uneducated woman, one who was not rich or politically powerful, could muster on no other basis than her own personal sanctity. We live in an age in which saints are no longer the heroes and heroines of our society. Our heroes and heroines are athletes who hit home runs or score touchdowns, singers who win gold records, entrepreneurs who make millions of dollars, and politicians who promise material abundance. To a large extent, this attitude is due to a change in values in society at large. Indeed, whereas in Catherine's time a life of holiness was something to talk about, our contemporaries are more interested in the lives of soap opera characters.

But this description does not give us the entire picture. Our age is still moved by the love and sacrifice of an Albert Schweitzer or of a Mother Teresa. Perhaps, rather than simply blaming our age, we ought also to look at ourselves, at the life of the church, and see if we too have been too quick in abandoning the ideals of holiness. Perhaps society no longer looks for saints because the church no longer looks for saints. Perhaps we are too much like those whom God described in Catherine's *Dialogue*. Perhaps we confuse material success with Christian obedience, eloquence with wisdom, appearance with reality. Perhaps what we need is to enter into a living dialogue with the living God, as Catherine did.

Second, a contemporary reader may be surprised at the way Catherine combined mysticism with activism. We, who usually consider ourselves to be so much wiser than the people of the Middle Ages, tend to divide mysticism and activism. We tend to think of a mystic as one who experiences an inner communion with God but knows little of what is going on in the world. We think of an activist as one who stands for justice and peace in the world but knows little of the inner peace of mystical experience. By our actions and our inner struggles and debates within the church, we imply that one must choose between evangelism and social action. We imply that if we are for justice in South Africa or for peace in Central America or for racial equity in the United States, we must not be very much interested in evangelism. And we imply that if we are for the good news, then we must play down all these other issues, as if they somehow obscure the nature of the gospel.

But Catherine—and Scripture—teaches us otherwise. The God whom she loved sent her out into the world. She was powerful in the world because of the power of her love for God. Love of God and love of society are not mutually exclusive. In fact, each requires the other. The good news of Jesus Christ is also news of peace and justice. True peace and justice are based on the action of God in Jesus Christ. To claim to love God and then fail to love the neighbor in concrete, social action is to be a liar. And to love the neighbor without loving God is to fall into idolatry.

---

[1]From *The Life of St. Catherine of Siena*, by Raymond of Capua; Part 2, Chapter 1.

[2]From *Epistle to Pope Gregory*, by Catherine of Siena.

[3]From *Dialogue*, by Catherine of Siena; Chapter 127.

[4]From *Dialogue*; Chapter 127.

6

A Piety of Vocation

Few major figures of the Roman Catholic Church are as well-known and as misinterpreted among Protestants as Ignatius of Loyola. Since he was the founder of the Jesuits and that order soon became the right arm of the Roman Catholic Church in its anti-Protestant polemics and policies, most Protestants have heard of him only as an archenemy or as a dogmatic and rigid man.

This picture of Ignatius, however, is far from accurate. Indeed, when one reads Ignatius's writings, one becomes strangely aware that his spiritual pilgrimage and struggles were very similar to Luther's and that in his understanding of vocation he was quite close to Calvin.

A Soldier's Pilgrimage

Ignatius was born of a noble Basque family at the ancestral castle of Loyola, just south of the Pyrenees. In contrast with Francis and Catherine, who gave signs of their religious vocation from their early years, Ignatius wished to become a famous soldier. He trained as such, and he participated in a war between Castile and Navarre that culminated in the siege of Pamplona. While participating in that siege in 1521, Ignatius received a wound that put an end to his dreams of military glory. Ignatius was bitterly disappointed. He was only twenty-six years old. His military career was about to bloom. But he had been shot in both legs, and his right leg did not heal properly. The bone had to be broken and reset in an excruciatingly painful procedure. He was bedridden in his ancestral home for months, and for the rest of his life he limped noticeably.

During his recuperation, Ignatius asked for something to read in order to pass the time. He was quite fond of novels of chivalry, a literary genre that was popular at that time and on which many of the more devout frowned. No such books were in the house, however. So, he was given a *Life of Christ* and a *Life of the Saints*. These two books made a big impression on Ignatius. He began to think that the principles they advocated offered him an alternate route to glory, now that his military endeavors were at an end.

After reading these books, Ignatius felt he was being pulled in two different directions. He had romantically and secretly devoted his knightly deeds to a lady of high birth whose identity is unknown. At times, in spite of his broken leg, he still dreamed of serving her. At other times, he considered imitating the great deeds of the saints about whom he was reading; and he would think "of going barefoot to Jerusalem and of eating nothing but grass."[1] But then something happened. As he wrote many years later (referring to himself in the third person),

Lying awake one night, he clearly saw an image of Our Lady with the Child Jesus, and this vision gave him great consolation. From that point he felt such repugnance for his past life, and especially for things of the flesh, that it was as if all the images that had been painted in his soul had been erased. So, from that very hour until August of '53, when this is being written, never again did he have the slightest inclination to things of the flesh. And this in itself shows that the thing was of God, although at the time he did not dare affirm it, but would only tell what had happened. Yet, his brother as well as all who lived there came to see outwardly the change that had taken place inwardly.[2]

Ignatius decided to go on pilgrimage to Jeruslem, but his brother would hear none of it. Ignatius's brother insisted that he should return to the duke in whose service he had been and seek a new form of service. Without letting his brother know of his resolve, Ignatius simply escaped from the house and took to the road that he hoped would lead him to Jerusalem. At that point in his life, as he later wrote, his goal was simply to imitate the outward actions of the saints, as he had previously tried to imitate the glorious deeds of knights, with little consideration for inner motivations.

Along the way, Ignatius purchased a long shirt of sackcloth. At the abbey of Montserrat (near Barcelona, Spain), he spent the night standing and kneeling in prayer before the altar of the virgin Mary.

The next morning Ignatius secretly gave his garments to a poor man and continued traveling south. The following day he was pursued and stopped by an officer who told him that the man to whom Ignatius had given his garments had been arrested for stealing them. The officer asked Ignatius to confirm the poor man's story. Ignatius did so.

The officer was quite impressed by Ignatius and spread the word that the man dressed in sackcloth was in truth a nobleman of holy life. Much to Ignatius's chagrin, this publicity made it impossible for him to continue his pilgrimage unnoticed. In any case, wishing to avoid the larger city of Barcelona, where there were many who knew him and his family, he went to the town of Manresa.

From Pilgrim to Saint

During the year he spent at Manresa, Ignatius underwent the struggle that would make him a saint. He heard a voice within his soul asking him if he could sustain this style of life for the seventy more years that he would have to live. Another voice responded, "How can you count on even one more hour of life?"[3] Doubts about himself and his own resolve began assailing Loyola. Like Luther just a few years earlier and half a continent away, Ignatius was deeply aware of his unworthiness. What Luther called his "anxieties," Loyola called his "scruples"; but the experience of despair in the midst of one's sinfulness was quite similar. Luther could well have written the following lines from Loyola's *Autobiography*:

At this point he came to suffer much from scruples. Although the general confession that he had made at Montserrat was very carefully done, . . . it still seemed to him sometimes that there were some things he had not confessed, and this caused him great affliction. Even if he then confessed those things, he still was not satisfied. He therefore sought out spiritual men who could offer a remedy for such scruples. But nothing helped. A certain Doctor Seo, a very spiritual man who preached there, told him one day in confession to write everything he could remember. This he did, and confessed it all; but the scruples returned, pressing him ever closer, so that he was in great tribulation. And, although he knew that such scruples were harmful, that he should be rid of them, he was unable to do so. Sometimes he thought that the best solution would be for his confessor to order him to forget about the past. He wished his confessor would do so, but he dared not ask for it. . . .

As such thoughts gripped him, he was often sorely tempted to jump through a window in his room, next to the place where he prayed. But, knowing that to take one's life was a sin, he would again cry: "Lord, I shall do nothing to offend Thee!"[4]

Clearly, what was taking place was that Ignatius had moved away from his shallow goal of imitating the deeds of the saints to a deeper understanding of the importance of inner motivations. Like Luther, when Ignatius examined his motivations and the actions stemming from them, he found himself wanting and fell into great despair. Also like Luther, he tried to punish himself. At one point he determined to fast until either his "scruples" were gone or he was on the verge of death. After a week of complete fasting, Loyola told his confessor what he was doing. His confessor ordered Ignatius to eat.

No remedy for Ignatius's turmoil seemed available. Then, unexpectedly and inexplicably, it happened. Ignatius gives us no details. He simply says that he began meditating on the "lessons that God had given him"[5] and came to the conclusion that he was forgiven, that it was no longer necessary to confess any of the things that had troubled him so much. "And thus from that day on he was free of those scruples, for he was certain that in his mercy God our Lord had wished to free him."[6]

The Pilgrimage Continues

Ignatius continued his journey to Jerusalem. Along the way, he made a stop in Rome. While there, he visited Pope Adrian VI. Again, the comparison with Luther is inevitable. Luther went to Rome in 1510, when the pope was Julius II, a man known more for his wars and his intrigues in Italian politics than for his pastoral concerns. The Rome that Luther saw was a city devoted to making money for Julius's wars and intrigues. Later, when Luther's protest began, the pope was Leo X, who was more interested in finishing the basilica of Saint Peter than in building up the church of God. In contrast, when Ignatius visited

Rome in 1523, he received the papal blessing. Adrian VI was a Dutchman inclined toward reform. Adrian had been a teacher of both Erasmus and Charles V, and many people hoped he would purify the church of its ills and corruption. This pope, who, unfortunately, died less than six months after Ignatius's visit, was able to understand and appreciate the zeal that moved Loyola.

When Ignatius finally arrived in Jerusalem, he decided to remain there, both in order to be able to pray for the rest of his life at the holy site and in order to convert the Turks. However, the Franciscans who worked in Jerusalem did not wish him to stay, probably because they feared that the zeal of this strange and theologically unlearned man would create difficulties with the Turks. Loyola insisted on staying; but the Franciscans told him that the pope had given them authority to command all Christians in the area, and they ordered him to leave. Obediently, Ignatius did so.

What was Loyola to do? Ever since his conversion, Ignatius's dream had been to go to Jerusalem. Now that was done. Loyola's voyage back to Spain was interrupted briefly near Genoa, where he was mistaken for a spy and temporarily imprisoned. But one can imagine that during the entire trip Ignatius's main concern must have been the future direction of his life. Perhaps he came to the conclusion that one of the reasons the Franciscans in Palestine had regarded him askance was his lack of theological training. In any case, by the time he reached Barcelona, he had determined that he would study.

By then, Loyola was about thirty years old—at that time an old age to begin studying. His fellow students were much younger than he. However, the depth of Ignatius's devotion profoundly impressed quite a few of them. Thus began gathering the nucleus of what would eventually become the Society of Jesus.

When Ignatius had studied for two years in Barcelona, his teachers told him that he was ready to move on to the University of Alcala, at that time one of the best schools in Spain. While Loyola was at Alcala, the group around him grew; and it also drew the attention of the Inquisition. The leaders of the Inquisition insisted that Ignatius and his followers could not wear a habit since they were not a recognized order. Ignatius and his followers obeyed.

Suspicion, however, was not allayed; and eventually Ignatius spent seventeen days in prison. But he remained firm in his beliefs, and after every inquiry the authorities absolved him. From Alcala, he went on to study in Salamanca and finally in Paris. In both cities the members of the Inquisition examined him.

The group that had gathered around Ignatius finally decided to make a solemn vow of poverty, of chastity, and of obedience to the pope. They also decided to go to the Holy Land to convert the Moslems. When they were about to depart, Ignatius heard that he had been accused once again before the Inquisition. This time he presented himself spontaneously before the inquisitor, who confirmed that Ignatius had indeed been accused and asked him for his writings. Ignatius complied by giving him a copy of his *Spiritual Exercises* (to which we will return later). The inquisitor was so impressed that he not only let Ignatius go but also asked for a copy of the *Exercises* for his personal use.

At this point, having made their vows at Montserrat, Ignatius and his friends had practically become a monastic order. However, becoming a monastic order required ecclesiastical approval. So, Ignatius and his companions traveled to Italy to seek the pope's blessing. They encountered many difficulties. They were repeatedly accused of heresy or of subversion. Finally, in 1540, Pope Paul III approved the new order, which was called the Society of Jesus, or, more commonly, the Jesuits. By then the challenge of Protestantism was such that responding to it became one of the Jesuits' major concerns.

However, the Jesuits never abandoned their missionary interest. A number of them did go to work among the Moslems. Quite soon, under the leadership of Francis Xavier, Jesuit missionaries were at work as far east as Japan and throughout the Spanish and Portuguese possessions in the Western Hemisphere.

The Spiritual Exercises

The debate regarding the anti-Protestant activities of the Jesuits has obscured much of the genuine piety of Ignatius. This piety is apparent in his autobiography but most especially in his *Spiritual Exercises*, a series of exercises in devotion that he composed as a result of his own experiences. These exercises are not easy. They require total concentration and usually take four weeks of retreat to complete.

What most strikes the modern reader of the *Exercises* is, first of all, their flexibility. Ignatius did not intend that all those who follow the *Exercises* come to the same conclusion or decision. He insisted in his instructions to spiritual directors that the various exercises must be adjusted according to an individual's age, education, and intelligence. While the exercises should normally take four weeks to complete, that time can be adjusted as necessary, taking into consideration an individual's state of soul and worldly responsibilities. Also, when going through the exercises, it is normally better for an individual to move away from home to a place of retreat where the matters of everyday life will not be an interruption. But if participants cannot do so, they may remain at home if they keep interruptions to a minimum.

Ignatius further insisted that spiritual directors must not go beyond making sure that participants understand the exercise. He also insisted that individuals be left free to reach their own conclusions. Furthermore, spiritual directors must take care not to promote the Jesuit or the monastic way of life or to make any other such decision for participants. On the contrary, the purpose of the *Exercises* is for the individual to seek and discover the divine will.

Ignatius believed that the notion of vocation was extremely important. He did not think that all are called to follow the way of life he followed. However, he did believe that all Christians must seek to discover God's will for them—their vocation in the strict sense. For Loyola, the word *vocation* clearly meant calling by God. In other words, the purpose of Ignatius's *Exercises* was to help people develop spiritually, not to recruit members for the Society of Jesus. In this regard Ignatius was close to Calvin and the entire Calvinistic tradition, which has also insisted on the need to discover what God is calling one to do. The same approach is part of the United Methodist tradition.

In reading the *Exercises*, one becomes quite aware of their emphasis on the senses. Ignatius leads the reader through a series of meditations on various points of the gospel and suggests that one *see* the people involved, that one *listen* to their conversation, that one *smell* and *taste*, that one *touch* the people and places. Naturally, one must have these experiences through the imagination, but one must attempt to make them as real as possible. For instance, Ignatius suggested that when one meditates on one's sins or on the suffering of Jesus Christ, one should be in a dark and somber place and that the opposite should be the case when one meditates on the Resurrection or on the joys of heaven. Even the temperature should be conducive to the proper mood, that is, appropriate for the subject on which one meditates. Thus, while Ignatius believed that the body and its passions must be kept in subjection, he did not think that one should seek to transcend the senses but rather to place them at the service of devotion.

The Christian spirituality Ignatius advocated has been called "joy in the world." Ignatian spirituality, in contrast with that which we studied in the first chapter of this book, was not one of flight from the world but one of rediscovering the world under a new light. When through the *Exercises* one learns to use the senses as a means to spiritual reflection, all that the senses perceive is viewed from the perspective of the divine purposes and is thus an occasion for further reflection.

A Piety for Today?

When one becomes acquainted with Ignatius's inner struggles, Loyola becomes a much more attractive figure than when one simply views him as the founder of the Jesuits and assigns to him the responsibility for all that they have done over the centuries. Like anyone today who takes faith seriously, Ignatius had to wrestle with himself, with the world, with the church, and even with God. He experienced high moments, but he also had to endure difficult and perplexing times, just as we do.

Ignatius's concern for vocation was particularly significant. Like us, he lived in a rapidly changing world. He was born just about the time when the travels of Columbus and others were opening new vistas and possibilities to Western Europe. This situation was particularly the case in his native Spain, where news and legends about the New World were avidly received. It was also true of Portugal, whose sailors had recently turned the Cape of Good Hope and opened trade with the Orient. For a Spaniard or for a Portuguese, the question of what one was to do with one's life was an open question, more open that it had been for centuries or was still in Germany, where one's station in life limited what one could do. Thus, while Luther was encouraging his followers to see the sanctity of the life in which they found themselves, Ignatius was calling his followers to discover where God wanted them to go. And go they did—to the New World, to India, to Japan, to the universities, to Germany.

Likewise, we need to see Ignatius's "joy in the world" in the context of an entire awakening of interest in the world of the senses that was sweeping through Western Europe. The Renaissance was part of this awakening; so was the new interest in scientific inquiry, culminating in the publication in 1543 of Copernicus's book titled *On the Revolutions of the Celestial Spheres* (a mere three years after the official founding of the Society of Jesus). This new interest in the world led many people to wordly pursuits and values. Other people rejected the world in the name of religion. Ignatius and his followers were vitally interested in the world, placed it under the perspective of divine creation and goodness, and developed a piety for the new age. It is no coincidence that many Jesuits, besides having sound theological training, hold doctorates in various secular fields.

People today are facing issues similar to those the people of Ignatius's time confronted. The vast number of choices open to us as we decide what we are to do with our lives increases the urgency for a piety that places the issue of divine calling at its very heart. In a world where so many possibilities exist that they baffle the imagination, there is only one way to find the right path. That way is to ask, "What does God call *me* to do?"

Likewise, we are living in times when the world fascinates us. Indeed, the world fascinates us so much that we are often tempted to tear it apart just to see how it works. Or, we are so attracted by the possibilities that the world offers some of us that we forget other values, particularly the needs of the rest of creation (as, for instance, when we argue that we should continue depleting the ozone in the atmosphere because to do so is good business).

Some Christians, perplexed by the complexity of these issues and by the difficult ethical choices that the modern world places before us, are tempted to retreat into a world-denying sort of religiosity. But we can learn from the piety that Ignatius showed forth. We can learn to look at the world, not as a field open to exploitation or as something to be dreaded, but as a means and a place in which to experience and serve God.

---

[1]From *Autobiography*, by Ignatius; Chapter 1.
[2]From *Autobiography*; Chapter 1.
[3]From *Autobiography*; Chapter 3.
[4]From *Autobiography*; Chapter 3.
[5]From *Autobiography*; Chapter 3.
[6]From *Autobiography*; Chapter 3.